CAMBRIDGE
1888-1988
IN PICTURES

CAMBRIDGE
1888-1988
IN PICTURES

Researched and compiled by
Michael J. Petty

Edited by Peter Wells,
assistant editor *Cambridge Evening News*

CAMBRIDGE NEWSPAPERS LIMITED

Published in 1988 by Cambridge Newspapers Ltd,
51 Newmarket Road, Cambridge CB5 ATJ

© Cambridge Newspapers Ltd, 1988

ISBN 0 902808 01 X

Designed by Kate Hughes-Stanton
Design and production in association with
Book Production Consultants,
47 Norfolk Street,
Cambridge CB1 2LE
Typeset by Omnia Limited
Printed and bound at the University Press, Cambridge

Contents

Acknowledgements

In selecting the illustrations for this book I have drawn upon four main collections. They are those of the Cambridge Antiquarian Society, Cambridge and County Folk Museum, Cambridgeshire Libraries and Information Service ('The Cambridgeshire Collection') and the *Cambridge Evening News* itself. I acknowledge my grateful thanks to them all and to the individuals charged with their administration and use.

Pictures are not taken by organisations but by individuals and amongst those featured within these pages are a veritable 'Who's Who' of the Cambridge photographic scene. Many of them are the work of professionals such as Ramsey and Muspratt, J Palmer Clarke, Scott and Wilkinson, Arthur Nichols, J B Hunt, Thomas Stearn and John Carter, along with Aerofilms of Boreham Wood, Messrs Valentine, Frith and other postcard companies. They are juxtaposed with photographs by talented amateurs, amongst whom are Percy North, Briscoe Snelson, William Tams, Ted Mott, Captain Hatfield, Charles Cudworth, Louis Cobbett and Matthew Mason. Many others are by photographers not individually named but I sincerely trust they would be delighted to know that their pictures snapped so long ago are now appreciated.

In addition there are drawings and engravings, including those of Arthur Moden and Frank Keene, whose humorous commentaries on the Cambridge of their day are still topical eighty years later.

On a personal note I wish to acknowledge the support and assistance shown to me by Cedric Tarrant and his award-winning team of photographers, along with Peter Wells and Bob Satchwell at the *Cambridge Evening News*.

To those individuals who during the last two years have shared with me the distinction of administering the Cambridgeshire Collection – Chris Jakes, Judith Wilson, Aysha Landesmann and Ruth Wilson – I owe sincere thanks and two assurances: any errors contained in this text are my own, and that my wife Patricia has endured even more with a dining room as full of paper as my desk at the library!

Preface

I am delighted to write a short preface to this splendid book. While it has, of course, been produced to mark the first century of the *Cambridge Evening News*, we are also publishing it very much in recognition of the strong and lasting links between the newspaper and the community it serves.

My family has been associated with the paper for more than a quarter of its first 100 years and my uncle, Lord Iliffe, who purchased it in 1959, has had an abiding affection for Cambridge since his undergraduate days at Clare College.

It is not difficult to understand why. Even during the last century of drastic change, the city has retained much of its charm and the university has continued to build on its reputation for academic excellence. Today more than at any time in the past, there is a vibrant spirit of co-operation between all who work and go about their daily lives in Cambridge. That is just how it should be and the *News* is proud to be part of it.

Michael Petty must be congratulated for his painstaking efforts, which so vividly recreate the last century. No-one can precisely predict the future for Cambridge, but our newspapers will do all they can to encourage the city's continued success.

Chairman, Cambridge Newspapers Ltd,
proprietors of the Cambridge Evening News

City Centre Changes

Cambridge is an amazing mixture of the familiar and the forgotten. Much of the change occurred in the inter-war years as colleges increased their student accommodation and large shops moved into the central area.

Market Hill: Two views from the spire of Holy Trinity Church, both taken within days of each other in 1901. *Far right:* Great St Mary's Church, King's College Chapel and the Old Schools, much as they are today. Only the tram lines in St Mary's Street, hansom cabs alongside the church and the absence of the Boer War memorial date the picture. *Right:* The same

location from a different angle. The south side of the Market Place being rebuilt for Guildhall expansion in the 1930s.

Below: The north side of Market Hill in 1935 showing demolition for new college rooms and shops erected by Gonville and Caius College. MacIntosh's on the other side of Rose Crescent was demolished and rebuilt in 1962.

Below right: The east side of Market Hill pictured in 1921 and showing the Victoria Cinema before it moved nearer the corner of Market Street in 1931. Underground toilets were built in 1902 and the fountain top removed in 1953 (part of it is now in the Folk Museum).

Peas Hill: The traditional site for the Saturday fishmarket until traffic forced it out. The last stall, that of Gustav David, moved in 1959 to his weekday spot on Market Hill.

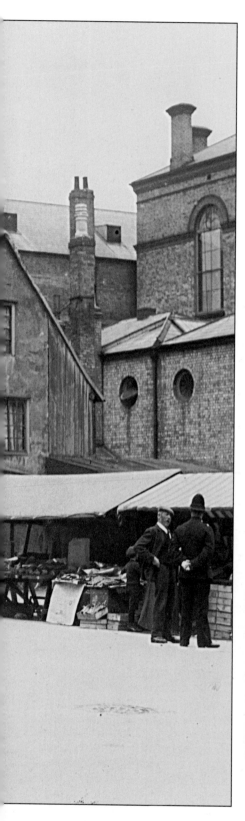

Overleaf: Fire destroyed the corn merchant's premises at the junction of Wheeler Street in 1904. Rebuilt in 1915, the rest of the east side *(left)* was demolished for the Guildhall in 1935. The old Central Hotel, demolished for a King's College hostel in 1960, can also be seen.

Above: The west side of Peas Hill in 1910. It was rebuilt from the corner of St Edward's Passage for more student accommodation in 1935.

The Market Square *(below)*: Until 1969 it was used as a carpark on weekdays with stalls around the outside.

Guildhall Street *(right)*: The buildings on the left, formerly the Castle Inn, were demolished when county and police courts were built in 1895.

Below: The other side of Guildhall Street, showing the Black Swan Inn (now Fisher House), which was converted in 1924 to house the chaplaincy to Roman Catholic undergraduates and escaped demolition for the Lion Yard scheme.

Petty Cury: Two views across the front of the Guildhall show how the area has changed beyond recognition. Nothing remains from the early picture. Chater and Osborne's shop on the corner was demolished in October 1889. The discovery of old stone fireplaces put the date of the building at 1538. Hallack and Bond's grocery shop took its place.

Far right: Petty Cury from the junction with Sidney Street. The Post Office building, erected in 1885, served until the present one opened in 1934. The buildings on the right were altered to make way for the expansion of Boots. Demolition began in March 1930. Unchanged is the location of the newspaper seller *(right)*. In earlier times one was arrested and fined for refusing an order from the police to quieten his call.

Petty Cury in 1909 *(below right)* and around 1960 *(below)*, showing little change, although some demolition, not shown here, had already taken place. One way traffic – with the exception of bicycles – was introduced in 1925.

PETTY CURY, CAMBRIDGE.

Cambridge, Petty Cury.

The south side of Petty Cury *(above & below)* saw extensive change even before the Lion Yard redevelopment. Protests were voiced in the 1870s, but demolition of the Wrestlers Inn *(right)*, described as 'a fine Jacobean building, perhaps the most striking and perfect of any of the old houses in Cambridge', followed the building of the Post Office.

Neighbouring small buildings were rebuilt in 1903. By the 1950s they had neat shop fronts but the upper storeys were condemned as fire traps.

Two streets opened off the south side of Petty Cury – one the former yard of the Falcon Inn *(right)*. The galleries were demolished in 1903 to allow expansion of the Lion Hotel, and the left side was rebuilt as offices in 1895. The other, Alexandra Street *(far right)*, built on the site of two inn yards in 1870, had lost its desirability as an address by about 1970 when the smell from MacFisheries permeated the area.

A painting made in 1926 from an upper window of the Downing Street laboratories *(below)* shows the maze of buildings which disappeared as areas were cleared for carparking before the redevelopment of Lion Yard.

E.T. TALBOT
1926

The old Corn Exchange at the junction of Downing Street and Corn Exchange Street *(below)*, which was made redundant in 1876 when the present building opened. From that time until 1884 it served as a covered market called the Cambridge Arcade. Later it was a variety music hall. But the popularity of night-time outdoor skating in the severe frosts of 1894–5 emptied it, even causing the cancellation of a Marie Lloyd concert. It was to be a cycle shop and then a garage before demolition in 1961.

Silver Street *(right)*: The buildings on the left were redeveloped in 1891, but the road was not substantially widened, and it was plagued by traffic as early as 1912.

Below: Across the bridge from Silver Street stood houses demolished by Queens College for Walnut Tree Court in 1935. Beyond is Newnham Grange, home of George Darwin (son of Sir Charles), which formed part of Darwin College in 1965.

Silver Street bridge was identified as a bottleneck. One suggestion in 1911 was for a new bridge across Mill Pool (right) from Silver Street to the Kings and Bishop Mill – demolished in 1927 – with a road along Coe Fen.

Below right: Rebuilding came in 1958. The demolition of the old bridge, dating from 1843, began with the erection of a temporary bridge. The new one was in place the following year.

St Andrews Street: Complaints about obstruction at the junction of Downing Street and St Andrews Street were voiced in 1905. At the root of complaints were hoardings around the old Bird Bolt Hotel *(below)*. The site was eventually occupied by the Norwich Union building *(right)* in 1910 – demolished just 60 years later.

Emmanuel Street *(far right)*: Plans to close the street and build a new road were blocked in 1901. Instead, an underpass was built linking new college development with the main building on the other side of the street.

Southgate Lodge and adjoining houses, built only 40 years before for Richard Rowe as an architect's office, were demolished in 1911. Demolition of property further along the street in preparation for redevelopment on the corner of St Andrews Street took place in 1955.

Bradwells Yard was demolished for the shopping arcade which opened in 1960, providing a link with Drummer Street Bus Station. Christ's Lane *(below right)*, with its barrier across the road, was closed.

St Andrews Street, Cambridge.

St Andrews Street *(left)*: Looking north from the junction with Emmanuel Street, the tall building glimpsed on the right was Rance's Folly. Built by Alderman Henry Rance, he held council meetings there in the dining room during his mayoralty in 1882. Later used as the Liberal Club, it was demolished in 1957.

Below: An open-top double-decker bus passes the junction of St Andrews Street and Hobson Street. The building on the junction with Sidney Street was rebuilt for Lloyds Bank in 1934.

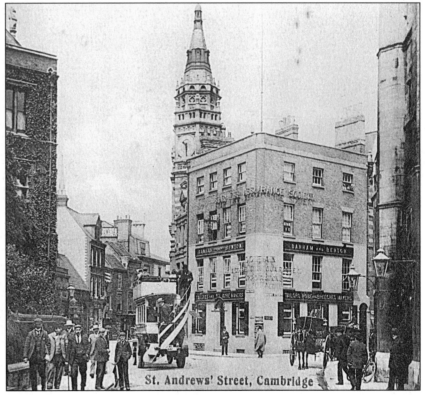

St. Andrews' Street, Cambridge

Sidney Street *(left)*: Both sides of the street were rebuilt during the 1930s as new shops moved into the area. The view from the junction with Petty Cury shows the buildings later demolished to make way for Boots.

Changes on the east side of Sidney Street, shown in 1901 *(above)*, began with the demolition in 1912 of the building occupied by Eaden, Spearing and Raynes (set back from the road and approached by a castellated archway). The neighbouring shops were rebuilt from 1931 *(below)*.

Market Street, Cambridge.

Market Street around 1930 *(above)*, and Sidney Street decorated for the Coronation of King George V in 1911 *(right)*, when Boy Scouts' founder, Baden-Powell, inspected Cambridge scouts. In 1931 he returned to the city to receive an honorary degree *(below)*.

Sussex Street *(above)*: Plans by the borough council to get the owners to widen the street and include a cinema fell through in 1920. In 1928, just a year after a buyer could not be found to take on the street for £20,000, Sidney Sussex College bought it. The south side was demolished and the new shops opened in 1932 *(below)*. Development of the north side followed in 1936.

Bridge Street/Round Church Street: Road widening in 1962 saw the end of Count Priziborksy's hairdressing shop *(right)*, one of the buildings which divided Round Church Street from Ram Yard. The count opened his shop in 1879 after being barber to the Imperial Austrian court. New development at the junction of the two streets in 1977 preserved and restored the old corner façade *(below)*.

Bridge Street/Magdalene Street around 1905 *(far right)*: Properties on the west side of Bridge Street were demolished in 1938 for St John's College residential accommodation. Similar buildings in Magdalene Street *(below right)* survived after a college plan to demolish the west side failed.

Magdalene bridge *(right)* gave the city – Cam Bridge – its name. The present bridge, opened in 1823, was restricted to 12-ton weights in 1953, and in 1967 was found to have a two-inch sag. It was preserved, strengthened and reopened by 1982 after proposals to rebuild failed in 1971.

Fisher Lane: Magdalene College rebuilt behind the frontages and demolished the houses in 1932 *(below)*. St. John's College completed the transformation with the Cripps Building *(above)* 1963-67.

Punting became popular in 1907. Fibreglass punts introduced in 1961 did not stand up to wear. Punt and punter could be

Castle Street, Cambridge.

hired by 1975 with the introduction of 'Chauffeurpunt'.

Buildings at the junction of Magdalene Street and Chesterton Lane (below) were demolished in 1912, although those on the west remained unchanged. The corner was widened in 1908, revealing the walls of the Olde White Horse Inn, shown here around 1920 (above). It became the Folk Museum in 1936.

All Saints Church, Cambridge.

St John's Street and Trinity Street: Dramatic changes in St John's Street – the demolition of the old All Saints Church *(left)* and the rebuilding of St John's College Chapel – took place in the 1860s. *Below:* Trinity Street, which appears largely unaltered, has seen major changes behind the frontages. Matthews, formerly the largest grocery shop in the city, was knocked down in 1969 to be replaced by a new Heffers shop and undergraduate rooms.

King's Parade in 1921 *(above right)* appears largely unchanged. But at this time the main bus terminus was opposite the Senate House.

The heavy railings *(below right)* – decorated for Queen Victoria's jubilee in 1887 – were removed in 1927 and replaced with others until 1932 when a wall was built. A major facelift to the shops opposite began in 1986.

Cambridge. Caius College and Senate House

A marked contrast in honorary degree ceremonies. *Above centre:* There was minimum security in Bene't Street in 1910 for Theodore Roosevelt, and the ceremony ended with a large teddy bear being dangled in front of the great man from a gallery of the Senate House. *Below right:* In 1975 police formed an impenetrable phalanx on either side of a procession which included the controversial General Gowon of Nigeria.

Above right: In 1892 the then Duke of Edinburgh received an honorary degree. Since 1977, the present Duke of Edinburgh has bestowed them in his capacity as Chancellor of the university.

Above left: In June 1888, the new *Cambridge Daily News* covered its first royal visit. The Prince and Princess of Wales arrived to see their son and heir, Prince Albert Victor, get his honorary degree. He had previously spent two years at Trinity College, during which time he was excused attendance at lectures.

In 1919, another Prince Albert, later to be King George VI, and Prince Henry attended the university. But the present Prince of Wales was the first 'royal' to earn a Cambridge degree in 1970 *(below far right)*. His youngest brother, Prince Edward, received his degree after spending three years at Jesus College.

University

Mortarboards and gowns still in evidence . . . but the mortarboards were abolished in 1953. In 1961 BAs were freed from wearing gowns after dark, and undergraduates followed suit in 1965. *Left:* Members of Christ's College Milton Society burn the 'damnable and dangerous' works of T S Eliot, a custom described as a 'traditional annual pilgrimage'.

The 'public school' image of the university has gradually dim-

inished, and in 1985 individual college entrance exams were scrapped to make way for new procedures designed to attract more State school entrants.

In 1911 a hundred horse-drawn and motor vehicles staged a mock funeral procession *(below)* for an undergraduate 'sent down' for a disciplinary offence. Others followed in 1912 and 1913. Despite moves to suppress them, another was held as late as 1962 when two students were 'sent down' for failing exams.

The winner of the wooden spoon – traditionally awarded to the mathematics graduate with the lowest pass – proudly displays his trophy. The custom continued until 1909.

Large crowds outside the Senate House *(below left)* await the outcome of a vote to see whether women undergraduates from the rapidly growing Newnham and Girton colleges should be awarded degrees. Proposals in 1897 and 1921 were both defeated.

Left: W E Gladstone planting a tree at Newnham College – it was later dug up by Tory undergraduates.

Far left: The Queen Mother, the first woman to be awarded a degree by the university after a change of rules in 1947. In 1954 New Hall opened the third foundation for women. Newnham College has elected to stay single-sex but Girton now admits men.

BITS OF OLD CAMBRIDGE

Nº 5. THE GIRTON GIRL

Topical Series—Published by the Cambridge Picture Post Card Co.

Restoration of St John's College gateway in 1934 *(right)*. Maintenance of old college buildings is an ongoing challenge.

King's College Chapel stonework needs constant attention. From 1961 Rubens' *Adoration of the Magi* was displayed for three years on a giant easel near the chancel screen *(left)* before being rehung in 1964 as an altarpiece. Major restoration finished in 1968 but by 1982 the chapel was again the subject of a restoration appeal.

A college development which went almost unnoticed in spite of its size . . . an aerial view of Trinity's Wolfson Building *(below)*, which provided 90 student bedrooms linked to commercial development, with Heffers and Sainsburys underneath in 1968. By 1986 further space was needed and the old Blue Boar vanished – with the exception of the Trinity Street frontage – to make room.

New college building boomed in the 1960s. The first stage of a new Fitzwilliam development was completed in 1963. Churchill College, named after Sir Winston, opened in 1964 with the former Prime Minister planting a tree *(below)*.

In 1981 the Queen opened Robinson College, founded and built with more than £18 million given by local millionaire recluse Sir David Robinson *(left)*. Darwin, founded in 1965, became the first graduate college in modern times. The increasing number of research students led also to the foundation of Lucy Cavendish, for graduate women, Clare Hall, University College (later to be renamed Wolfson) and Leckampton House (accommodation provided by Corpus Christi for its graduate students).

Right: The University Library nearing completion in 1934. Funded by a Rockefeller Foundation grant of £700,000, it was built in response to a major re-organisation of university teaching methods which included the introduction of the Faculty system where undergraduates from various colleges are taught together. Later came the award-winning History Faculty Library *(below right)*, so dogged by problems that it came close to demolition in 1984 but was finally extensively repaired.

Science

Of even greater significance has been the growth of science, described in 1919 as the 'greatest fact in the history of the University since its foundation'. Two acres were bought by the university as the nucleus of the Downing Site *(left)*, with a new botany and medical school and the Sidgwick Museum, opened by the King in 1904.

Research at the Cavendish lab *(below left)*, on the New Museums site, won Nobel prizes in 1904, 1906 and 1908 and here in 1932 two Cambridge scientists split the atom. Computers were developed at the Mathematical Laboratory from the 1930s; by 1949, EDSAC, the world's first electronic stored-programme automatic digital computer, was in operation *(below centre)*. Nobel prize winners Crick and Watson *(above far left)* used it in their DNA researches. Less than ten years later EDSAC II had cut problem solving from an hour to a minute.

It was clear by the mid-1960s that the city-centre sites were inadequate and in 1973 the New Cavendish Laboratory *(inset)* was built on the 300 acre site west of Cambridge, where other faculty buildings and the Mullard Radio Astronomy Laboratory had already been established.

Industry

Recent decades have seen increasing collaboration between Cambridge research and industry. The Cambridge Instrument Company *(right)* was founded as early as 1881 to manufacture the specialist equipment scientists demanded. After financial problems in the 1970s it is again in the forefront of its field.

Pye: A back garden in Humberstone Road in 1896 saw the start of the Pye group. Putting to use experience at the Cambridge Instrument Company and the Cavendish Laboratory, founder W G Pye started making apparatus for school laboratories and elementary university classes.

A move to Mill Lane in 1902 was followed by the opening of a new scientific instrument works in Newmarket Road in 1913. From making gun-sights in the First World War, the company switched in the post-war recession to radios *(above)* and, later, radar.

The founding of Pye Telecom in 1944 and amalgamation with Unicam, established in 1933, led eventually to the development of

scientific instruments for the first UK satellite and the opening of a joint scientific instrument centre in 1962. The company was the largest television manufacturer in Britain by 1952, but Government delays over the introduction of colour television and other problems led to a take-over by Philips in 1967. By 1987 the Pye name had vanished from Cambridge.

Sinclair: Clive Sinclair *(above far right),* later Sir Clive, arrived in Cambridge in 1966 and quickly set about building his reputation for innovation. Two mercurial decades have seen the introduction of pocket calculators, digital watches, small-screen television *(above right)* and cheap home computers.

Three years after the rescue of Sinclair Radionics by the National Enterprise Board in 1976, Sir Clive left the company and began Sinclair Research in Cambridge.

The launch of the ZX80 personal computer and other work was followed by the ill-starred C5 bicycle, and by 1985 computer marketing rights were sold to Amstrad. In 1986 Sir Clive launched two new companies, Anamartic and Moduliser.

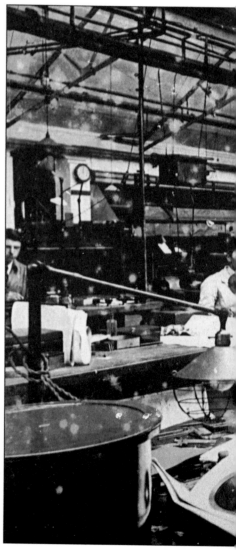

Acorn: Founded in 1979 by Chris Curry, Acorn Computers *(below)* linked with the BBC to produce computers for schools. In 1981 it bought Torch Computers, and in 1984 won the Queen's Award for Industry. After being hit in the micro-computer war it was rescued by Olivetti, and Curry left in 1986.

The rapid growth of new technology industry – dubbed the Cambridge Phenomenon – began with the opening of the city's Science Park in 1975 *(left)*.

Planning restrictions hampered earlier attempts at industrial expansion. In 1954 the county development plan discouraged large-scale production industry development. Trinity Hall Farm estate, designated in 1962, was restricted to companies displaced by council redevelopment.

Following a report in 1968 calling for the development of science-based industry, Trinity College identified the Science Park site. By 1982 it was estimated that there were 250–300 computer-based new technology companies in the area.

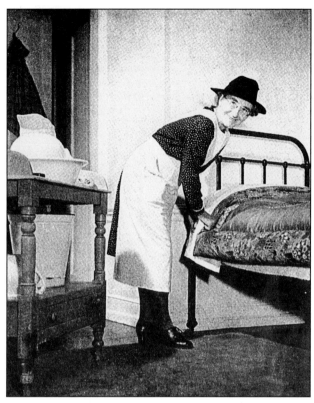

Cambridge still has its traditional jobs sector. The university was seen as a major employer of people like the 'bedder' *(left)*. A college servants' pay dispute in 1951 led to a 'charter' being drawn up, and pay for bedmakers rose the following year from 2s. 10d. to 3s. 6d. an hour.

Printing and the book-selling trade have provided hundreds of jobs. In 1984 Cambridge University Press celebrated 400 years of printing.

Unemployment in Cambridge became critical after the First World War. In 1921, with 721 jobless, schemes were initiated to employ 263. Some employed on relief work went on strike in 1923 as they were not getting Trade Union rates.

The construction of new roads was a favourite project. In 1926 the Coe Fen Road scheme found work for 90 men.

Earlier, in 1916, booksellers C P Porter and Leavis helped one jobless man by providing a barrow and books which he sold at one shilling apiece.

Best known of the booksellers was Gustav David *(below)*, who set up his stall in Market Hill in 1896. The same year saw Heffers open in Petty Cury, with Bowes and Bowes – now Sherratt and Hughes – arriving on the scene in 1899.

The problems of finding work continued into the 1930s. More road construction relief schemes were started, including new paving along the Backs. An appeal by the Mayor raised £1,122 for the unemployed within two weeks.

A reduction in the jobless total came with the Second World War. Large numbers of men were called up for military service, and the establishment of regional government at Brooklands Avenue increased jobs there by 350 per cent.

Some companies with a long tradition of Cambridge trading have vanished during the century. W K Bird and Son, vinegar works, closed in 1915 after 108 years. H J Gray, which celebrated its centenary in 1955, stopped volume production of wooden squash rackets in 1985, and left in 1986. Baldry's, established in 1923, took over Barker and Wadsworth, whose earliest factory is illustrated here, and moved to Sawston in 1979 before liquidation in 1982.

Others, like D MacKay Engineering, set up in 1912, continue to thrive.

ADSWORTH,
ublished 1818.

GTON STREET, CAMBRIDGE.
REW'S STREET, MILDENHALL.

Housing

In 1888 building was in full swing in New Chesterton, Cherry Hinton and Newnham. But the new housing was too expensive for most and as old homes disappeared families were forced to the workhouse or into sharing a home with as many as three other families.

1920 saw completion of the first block of post-war Corporation houses in Stanley Road and the start of a borough housing scheme with 100 homes built in Cavendish, Hills and Hinton avenues.

Tenants' Petition to Town Council

Photos   'Cambridge Daily News.'
Views of Gothic Street (above) and Doric Street (below).

CAMBS. DIVISIONAL   PETTY   SESSIONS

"APPALLING LIVING CONDITIONS"

Council homes in Milton Road *(above left)* were offered for sale at £579, with £5 down and the balance in weekly instalments of £1.1s.1d. (£1.05).

The tenants of Gothic Street and Doric Street *(below left)* drew up a petition against demolition of their homes, shown again right, to make way for new building.

Earlier, Cambridge Housing Society built 22 houses in Green End Road *(below)* for families who could not afford council rents of 7s. 3d. a week (about 36p). And the Hundred Houses Society was formed in 1933 to provide cheap houses to rent. By 1953 there was a 15-year waiting list for council houses.

The huge Arbury housing estate began to grow on former small-holding and poultry farmland *(left)* in 1956. 1965 saw the final phase of 'the Arbury', seen here under flood water.

By the 1960s, houses built 30 years earlier needed improvement. Later, in 1968, large scale slum clearance began in the Kite area.

A continuing shortage of accommodation saw 'squatting' become commonplace. Squatters moved into houses in John Street *(right)*.

The early 70s brought plans for huge development in Cherry Hinton, where residents had bemoaned urbanisation as early as 1896, and later in Ditton Lane and King's Hedges. The growth of high-tech industries has added the pressure of high prices to the housing problem.

Local Government

In 1912 Chesterton *(below & bottom)* and Newnham, after protest, were brought within the city boundary. Cherry Hinton *(below right)* and Trumpington *(right & far right)* followed in 1934.

The start of better relations between 'town and gown' was seen in 1889, with the appointment of six town councillors from the university and colleges. An attempt to gain county borough status was defeated in 1914, much to the indignation of the *News*. In 1951 the King granted Cambridge city status.

Charming Cambridgeshire
OLD CHESTERTON. *CAMBRIDGE*

Victoria Rd., Cambridge

Sergeant-at-Mace, Ken Quick, seen here on his retirement, with the Mayor, Coun. John Woodhouse, and predecessors, was a stalwart of the city council for 25 years.

County councils were established in 1888, to succeed Justices of the Peace. The JPs Assize Court on Castle Hill *(right)* was seen by the new council as being too far removed from the town centre.

Offices were rented throughout Cambridge, with meetings held in the Guildhall. After rejection of plans for a new joint headquarters with the town council, the county bought the Hobson Street Methodist Chapel, which was rebuilt as County Hall in 1913.

By 1932 the need for more space saw the Shire Hall built on Castle Hill *(below)*.

Plans for a new Guildhall *(below)*, rejected in 1897, surfaced again in 1932. Work began on the first phase *(above)* in 1935. Down came the old Shire House (1747) and the old Guildhall (1782). Completion came in 1939, but the official opening was abandoned at the outbreak of the Second World War.

The central library in Wheeler Street, seen below in 1930, became too small to cope with demand, and the new central library opened in 1975 as part of the Lion Yard development. The first branch library, at Mill Road *(above)*, opened in 1897.

Education

The 1902 Education Act gave borough councils control of the old Church schools like St Matthews, seen here in 1909, which led some Passive Resisters to refuse to pay the education rate. Following disputes between 1964 and 1972 over the abolition of the 11-plus examination and introduction of comprehensives, Parkside became the first community college, followed by Coleridge (*far right*). In 1974 the Cambridgeshire High Schools for Girls and Boys became Long Road and Hills Road Sixth Form colleges.

A grant of £100 in 1889 saw the start of what is now Cambridgeshire College of Arts and Technology (*below right*). It built a small institution in East Road for technical education. The Collier Road site opened in 1909, and the 1920s saw continual growth and the appearance of full-time students. By 1985 the debate had begun over whether CCAT should be granted polytechnic status.

The Roger Ascham school, closed in 1987, began life in 1916 as the Cambridge Open Air School for children suffering from tuberculosis, moving to Ascham Road in 1928.

The Perse School for Boys (*below far right*) was 275 years old by the time it moved from a site in Free School Lane in 1890 and again in 1960 to Hills Road. Other private schools include those of King's and St John's colleges, originally solely involved with the education of choristers.

A classics master at the Leys School, W Balgarnie (1900–51) was the basis for 'Mr Chips'. St Mary's Convent, now St Mary's, was founded in 1898 when nuns at York were sent to Cambridge to teach.

Religion

Long before education was compulsory Sunday schools were a means of education. Jesus Lane Sunday school was established to carry Christian teaching into the streets of Barnwell. By 1952, with every church having its own Sunday school, its work was finished.

The Theatre Royal Barnwell Mission *(left)*, established in what is now the Festival Theatre workshop in Newmarket Road, proved a major attraction until its demise during the First World War. The Salvation Army's founder, General Booth, visited Cambridge in 1907 – seven years before the 'Sally Army' opened its Citadel in Tenison Road in 1914 *(below left)*.

St Philip's Church *(right)* was built in 1889 to meet the demands of an expanding population. The massive Roman Catholic Church of Our Lady and the English Martyrs, seen here under construction, was consecrated in 1890.

Health

Dredger on R. Cam, Cambridge

Smoky Cambridge, seen *(right)* from the top of St John's College Chapel in 1903, changed with the introduction of smoke control orders in the 1960s.

Until 1895 sewage was dumped untreated into the Cam. By 1916 Cheddars Lane pumping station *(below right)* was already over-loaded, and in 1968 the new Riverside station was opened. The old works now house the Museum of Technology.

Flooding in the city was common in the early part of the century. Between 1914 and 1919 there were four floods, and the river was dredged *(above)* in 1923 and again in 1933 when enough silt was removed to cover Parker's Piece to a depth of nearly seven feet. Floods struck again in 1926, 1947 (shown here) and 1959. In 1978, as the Cam again overflowed its banks, experts warned 'we can never be safe'.

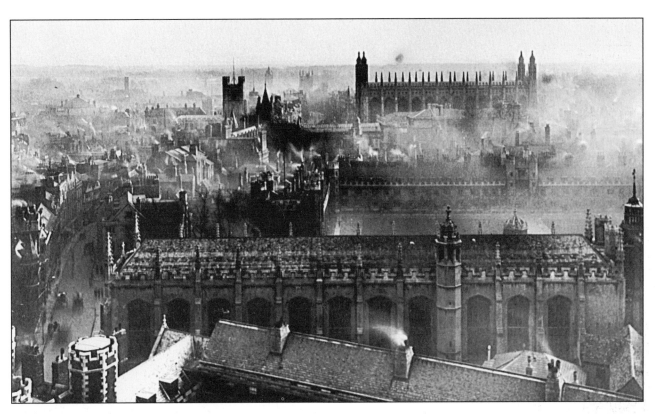

Health problems continued, with one in eight infants under 12 months dying in 1908. Cambridge became the first town to give proper attention to children's teeth. In 1911 a pasteurised milk depot for infants was opened, but there were delays the same year in the introduction of galvanised dustbins *(below right)* as the authorities feared they would be used as baby baths. Public baths were opened in Gwydir Street in 1927.

Fulbourn Water-works

Water: Fulbourn waterworks (*above*) and another supply from Cherry Hinton were shut down with the opening of a new well and pumping station at Fleam Dyke in 1921. This was operated by steam until 1976 when it was converted to electricity.

Other water supplies date back centuries. Trinity College fountain is fed by pipes from Conduit Head Road, which were laid by monks in 1325. Channels along Trumpington Street carry water from Nine Wells, which originally fed Hobson's Conduit, established on Market Hill in 1614. The fountain which replaced it had its decorative top removed in 1953 (part of the top is now in the Folk Museum).

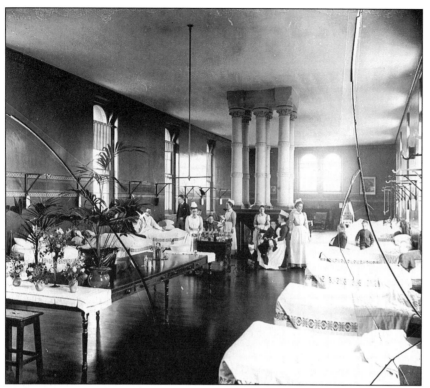

Addenbrooke's Hospital: Until 1903 admission to old Addenbrooke's Hospital *(left)*, closed in 1984, was on the recommendation of a governor. Contributions of 2d. a week ensured free treatment. The collectors are shown overleaf.

The hospital got an operating theatre in 1897, pathological labs in 1914, and a nurses' home with money collected for a war memorial in 1918. The open colonnades shown below in 1911 were enclosed in 1938.

The first stage of New Addenbrooke's Hospital was opened by the Queen in May 1962 *(right)*. The second stage was completed ten years later *(below right)*. The hospital has pioneered many medical advances. Kidney and liver transplants attracted world attention. In 1984, two-year-old Ben Hardwick's need for a liver transplant brought heavy media coverage.

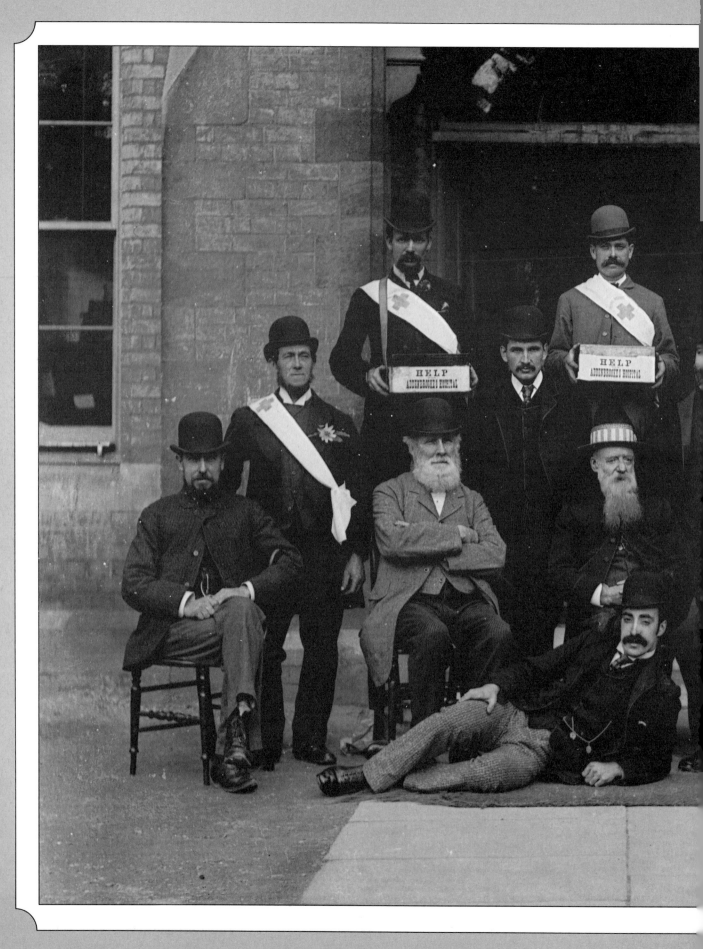

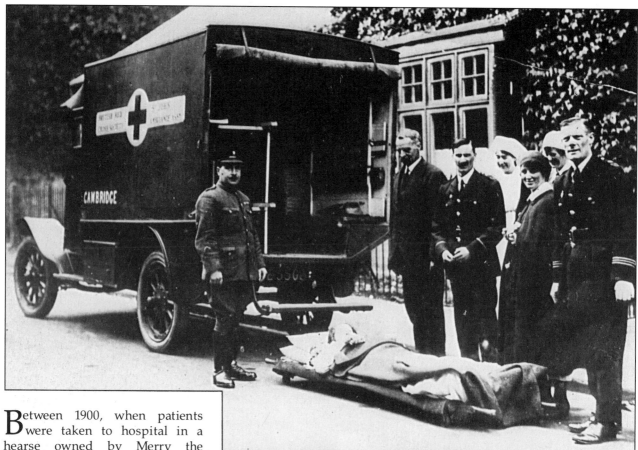

Between 1900, when patients were taken to hospital in a hearse owned by Merry the undertaker, and 1947, when Cambridgeshire ambulance service became the first to carry patients free of charge, ambulances supplied by the special constabulary and the Red Cross – like the one shown above outside Thompson's Lane nursing home – charged 1s. 3d. a mile (about 6p).

The nursing home was replaced in 1921 when Charles Agnew built the Evelyn Nursing Home, now the Evelyn Hospital (right), in Trumpington Road. It was named after his wife. More recently, a new private hospital has opened at Impington.

Far right: Staff outside the former Mill Road maternity hospital, which began life as a workhouse and established one of the finest reputations in the country despite the inadequacies of the building. It was replaced in 1983 with the Rosie Maternity Unit, paid for by Sir David Robinson and named after his mother.

Caring for the city's elderly has come a long way since the introduction of old-age pensions in 1908, when 500 aged poor could apply for 5s. a week (25p) 'for nothing'. Chesterton Hospital (*above*) is a far cry from the dreary Victorian institution it once was. Elsewhere, charities and institutions have helped. The Victoria Friendly Society's almshouses were established in 1891, and in 1957 Princess Margaret opened Langdon House.

Despite best endeavours the problems of homelessness and alcoholism remain part of the Cambridge scene, though no one has matched the 113 city court appearances of Trevor Hughes (*below*) before his death in 1978.

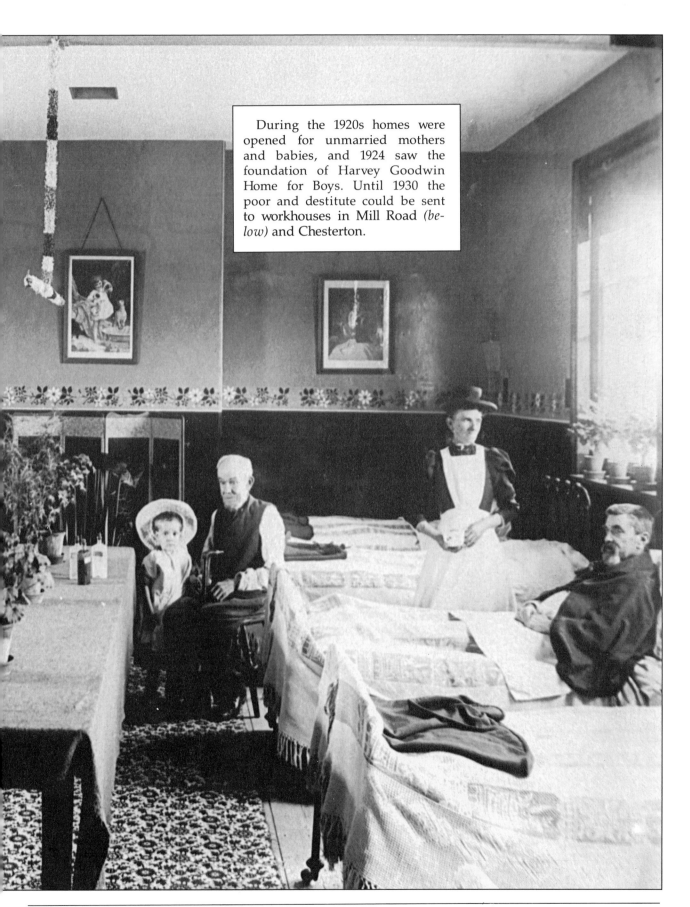

During the 1920s homes were opened for unmarried mothers and babies, and 1924 saw the foundation of Harvey Goodwin Home for Boys. Until 1930 the poor and destitute could be sent to workhouses in Mill Road *(below)* and Chesterton.

Leisure

Time has been called on many city pubs during the century, including The True Blue, Sidney Street (1919); The Three Tuns, Castle Street, shown above around 1900 (1936); the Criterion in Market Passage (1968) and the Bun Shop, St Andrew's Hill (1975). New pubs like the Milton Arms (1930) and the British Queen in Histon Road (1933) were opened to cater for the expanding population. The first new pub built after the Second World War was the Weathervane in Perne Road in 1959 (renamed the Master Mariner in 1983).

Breweries, too, have shut. The Panton brewery, shown here in 1910, was among nearly 20 which have disappeared. Others included Dales, which won 20 medals for its beer, Bailey and Tebbutt, Scales, Hudsons and The Star. But in 1984 the new Ancient Druids pub in Napier Street included an in-house brewery.

Larks – or beans – on toast: Towards the end of the Edwardian era a group of 'young gentlemen' at 20 Trinity Street dined on 'larks on toast using silver cutlery brought with them at the beginning of term' *(above)*. College tea was served just after 4p.m. with crumpets and muffins still hot from Matthews bakery. In 1942 the prestigious Pitt Club was taken as the base for a British Restaurant, dispensing plain fare for ordinary folk. After the war the Civic Restaurant operated from the old Post Office in Petty Cury until 1972 *(below)*.

Hotels: Two views of the Lion Hotel, where public dinners became famous after being taken over by Mrs A A Moyes in 1894. A glass roof was erected over the court *(above left)*, used by traffic until 1907. Closure came in 1963 and demolition *(below left)*, to make way for the Lion Yard, in 1969. In 1965 the University Arms opened a 200-bed extension; and after a disastrous fire in 1971, which meant a £2 million rebuilding programme, the Garden House reopened in 1973.

Other hotels have vanished, like the Central in Peas Hill, the Bull in Trumpington Street and the Castle Inn in St Andrews Street *(above)*, which was destroyed by fire in 1934. In 1986 the Blue Boar was closed by Trinity College to make way for student accommodation.

Cinemas: The Regal Cinema was a latecomer on the Cambridge scene when it opened in 1937. The first film had been shown in 1896 at Tudors Circus, later renamed The Hippodrome, on Auckland Road. The first cinema was the Empire in Mill Road, later the Kinema, in 1910. A year later the County Rink, re-named the Rendezvous and Rex, opened in part of a roller-skating rink. But the Playhouse in Mill Road was the first purpose-built picture house in 1912.

The first central cinema, the Electric Theatre (later re-named the Victoria) opened on Market Hill in 1911 and moved to the corner of Market Street in 1931, where it remained until its closure in 1988. The first talking picture, *Broadway Melody,* was screened in 1929 at the Central in Hobson Street *(right)*. It became a bingo hall in 1972.

Theatre: Until 1894 the University had power to prevent plays during term time. When the New Theatre *(right)* opened on St Andrews Street in 1896, undergraduates played a large part in its life, and were often ejected for bad behaviour *(far right)*. From 1933 the theatre showed films interspersed with variety shows. November 29, 1954, saw 'Jimmy Young and Variety' on the bill *(far right)*. The theatre was demolished in 1962.

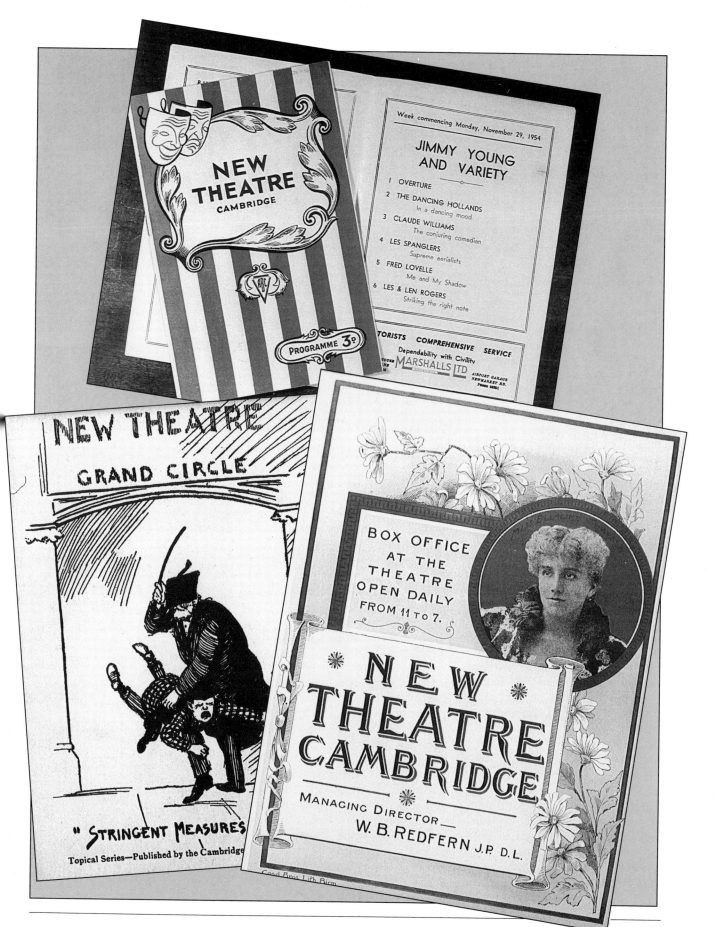

83

Festival: In 1926 Terence Gray started the Festival Theatre in the old Barnwell Theatre Royal building *(above centre)* on Newmarket Road, with the ambition of making it the most progressive in the country. New styles of sets, pioneering development in stage lighting, and programmes printed in white on transparent paper so they could be ready by the stage lighting were among the innovations. After Gray left in 1933 the theatre limped on for a year before closing. It later became the Arts Theatre workshop and the base of the Prospect Theatre Company, Britain's leading touring group between 1964 and 1977 *(below right)* .

Arts: Economist John Maynard Keynes paid for the Arts Theatre, which opened in 1936 as an entertainment venue for 'town and gown'. It continued to prosper under the chairmanship of Dr George 'Dadie' Rylands, who assumed the office after Lord Keynes' death in 1946 and con-

tinued at the helm until 1982. His retirement was marked by a recital at the Barbican by some of the biggest names in showbusiness grateful for their start in Cambridge. In 1986 the élite of the acting world, watched by Prince Edward *(above)*, gave a unique Shakespeare performance to celebrate the theatre's 50th birthday.

ADC: When Rupert Brooke appeared at the ADC Theatre in 1906 it had already been open for 51 years. The city's oldest theatre, Cecil Beeton helped there in the 1920s and spy Guy Burgess designed sets in 1931 for a production starring Sir Michael Redgrave. After a fire in 1933 it reopened in 1935. From 1964 the university helped with funding, and leased and managed the premises. *Above far right:* In 1985 members of the royal family attended a performance in which Prince Edward appeared, following the example set by Prince Charles in 1969 *(far right)*.

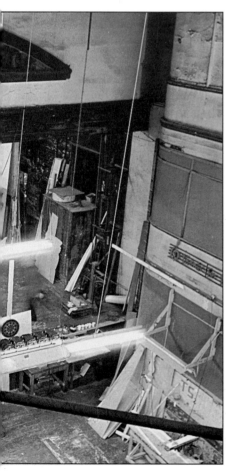

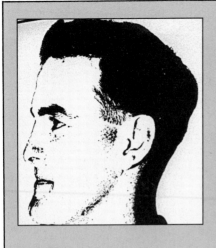

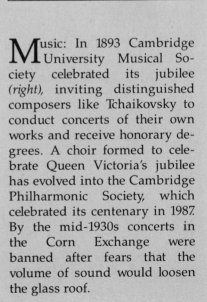

Household names in entertainment started in Footlights, the university revue company. Jack Hulbert appeared in 1913, Norman Hartnell in his own women's costumes (1921-3). Tim Brooke-Taylor *(top right)*, John Cleese *(top left)*, Bill Oddie *(above)*, Clive James and David Frost are ex-Footlight entertainers. Rescued from bankruptcy in 1932, Footlights became more professional and in 1963 its 'Cambridge Circus' went to London, Australia and New York.

Music: In 1893 Cambridge University Musical Society celebrated its jubilee *(right)*, inviting distinguished composers like Tchaikovsky to conduct concerts of their own works and receive honorary degrees. A choir formed to celebrate Queen Victoria's jubilee has evolved into the Cambridge Philharmonic Society, which celebrated its centenary in 1987. By the mid-1930s concerts in the Corn Exchange were banned after fears that the volume of sound would loosen the glass roof.

THE JUBILEE CELEBRATION OF THE CAMBRIDGE UNIVERSITY MUSICAL SOCIETY: SOME OF THE EMINENT COMPOSERS AT THE CONCERT IN THE CAMBRIDGE GUILDHALL.

AFTER A 'CONVERSATIONE' IN THE FITZWILLIAM MUSEUM 1893

THE NEW
DOROTHY CAFE-RESTAURANT

The Magnificent Ball Room, arranged as a Tea Room.

The Main Luncheon Room.

Byzantine Banqueting Hall—Overlooking Sidney Street.

Small Room arranged for Committee or Club Dinner.

One of the Oak Rooms arranged for a Wedding Reception.

The Dorothy Café and restaurant, a noble building which for two years and more has kept Cambridge people on the watch to realise assume its full measure, is completed.

During a period of unparalleled transformation among the old premises of the town, it is most distinctive, compelling attention, and, as the headquarters of a business which has been established nearly 100 years, is quite dignified and imposing. It is a building which justifies the proud satisfaction of Messrs. H. & P. Hoskins, Ltd. From an artistic point of view it is sufficient to remark of the merit that its erection has been commended by the Council of the Cambridge Preservation Society.

That so far as possible local labour was employed throughout is another attribute. Messrs. Forbes and Tate, F.F.R.I.B.A., of 97, Jermyn Street, London, were the architects, and Messrs. Coulson and Son, Ltd., of Cambridge, the general contractors. The furnishing was entrusted to Messrs. Robert Sayle and Co., Ltd., and Messrs. W. Stockbridge and Sons.

This palatial café-restaurant has a total accommodation of about 1,500. The decorative schemes, contrasting pleasantly as one ascends from floor to floor, are superb, while the barrel roof of the Banquet Hall and the vaulted ceiling of the restaurant are unique. The electric passenger lift brings all floors and the basement within effortless access.

Lighting and ventilation methods, all-important considerations, are noticeably effective. There are windows on each side of every

(Continued on page 10).

Another View of the Oak Rooms extended for Large Dinner Party.

The same room arranged for Smaller Party.

Dancing: The versatility of the Corn Exchange was demonstrated as early as 1904 when it could be converted for a ball at a cost of several thousand pounds. From time to time a bridge was built across Wheeler Street (*above*) linking it with the Guildhall for larger events. By 1931 Percy Cowell and his players were delighting up to 450 dancers at the New Dorothy Café-Restaurant (*left*). It remained an entertainment venue until its closure in August 1972.

The Beatles (*right*), 'a four-man rock group with weird hairstyles as a gimmick sang and played their current hits "Love Me Do" and "Please, Please Me". The fast-moving show was not the best Cambridge audiences have seen', said the *News*. Nine months later, in November 1963, the four lads returned to the Regal Cinema under police escort to entertain an ecstatic audience of 4,000. Just

seven years earlier the 'jive' had been banned in city dance halls. The ban lasted a year until the Rex ballroom allowed rock and roll sessions.

Cambridge street entertainment gained a national reputation in 1978 with the appearance on tele-vision of Michael Copley and Dag Ingram, the Cambridge Buskers. Within the Lion Yard they faced competition from others like Jerry Bol, briefly arrested during a time when the city council was rethinking its policies on street music.

The city's commons, originally grazing land for cattle and horses, have become popular recreation grounds. The Royal Show in 1894 *(above far right)* was the biggest event ever held on a common. Newly planted trees alongside Victoria Avenue were dug up and replanted later to prevent them from being crushed by the crowds. A bandstand put up for the event was transferred to Christ's Pieces, where it stood until 1956.

Midsummer Fair being opened in June 1972 by the then Mayor of Cambridge, Coun. Peter Wright *(above)*. Probably one of the best-known fairs in the world, it has long been associated with the Thurston family of showmen. However, Stourbridge Fair, once one of the greatest trading fairs in Europe, had declined in importance and it was abolished in 1934. Another traditional event, Reach Fair in the village of Reach 15 miles north-east of Cambridge, has continued uninterrupted.

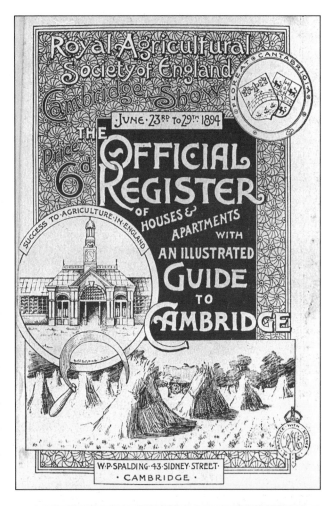

Circus: A sight no longer seen in Cambridge . . . elephants from Billy Smart's Circus parade through the city centre in 1971 (*left*). Ten years later the city council banned acts involving animals. In 1888 Keith and Tudors circus was fined for overstaying its time, and set up a permanent building in Auckland Road in 1896. Eight years later Buffalo Bill's Wild West Show visited the city.

Good Friday skipping on Parker's Piece (*above*) was a familiar sight until 1948 when only three groups took part. The custom was revived in 1987 by BBC Radio Cambridgeshire. Ninety years earlier the Piece was the scene of a huge dinner-party for old people to celebrate Queen Victoria's jubilee.

The internationally known service of nine lessons and carols at King's College Chapel (*right*) began in 1918. First broadcast in 1928, it missed the following year, but has been heard on radio ever since and been televised since 1963.

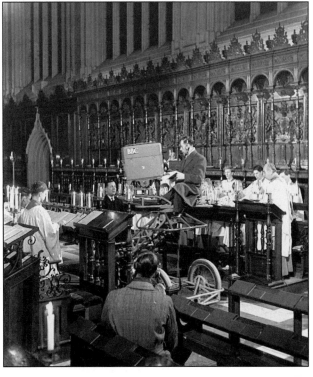

Visitors to Cambridge

An Esperanto Congress held in 1907 dwarfed all other events at that time. Market Hill was bedecked with flags (*left*). By 1926 more than 1000 were attending summer schools and conferences during August, like the gathering of Oddfellows shown below left.

Tourism was recognised in Cambridge as early as 1912 when the suggestion was made that it should be advertised like a seaside town. The Festival of Britain in 1951 encouraged the setting up of an information bureau in the library. By 1969 King's College was being forced to control visitors. The appointment of a tourist officer in 1973 was followed by the formation of official Blue Badge tourist guides.

The Backs *(left)*, always a tourist attraction, have changed dramatically in the past 40 years with the loss through disease of many giant trees such as those in avenues at Trinity and St John's. Others came down in 1975 and in the hurricane-force winds of 1987. Although replanting has taken place it will be many years before the trees reach maturity.

Queen Mary *(right)* was among a number of royal visitors to the city. She would visit Woolston's antique shop unannounced, arriving by car. One visit in 1934 made international news. The Queen's car broke down at Waterbeach, and a passing motorist, Mr Titmous, gave her a lift into Cambridge.

One of the most significant visits came in 1951, when the owner of the *Cambridge News*, Captain Taylor, became the first Mayor to welcome George VI *(left)* to the *city* of Cambridge following the grant of this status by the King. Two years later motorists were asked to stay away from Market Hill so their cars did not interfere with Coronation pictures being shown on four foot television screens in the Guildhall.

Transport

Cambridge railway station *(left)* was built far from the town centre in 1845 because of university objections to the railway line coming within a mile of its buildings. This led to a need for transport from the station. After the successful introduction of horse-drawn trams *(below)*, Cambridge Omnibus Company began a horse-drawn bus service in 1896 *(below left)*. The rival Cambridge Street Tramways Company countered the move with buses, and by 1902 the Omnibus Company went out of business. Its depot on Chesterton Road is now Frost's Garage.

AN ELECTRIC SHOCK.
A recent suggestion to electrify the horse-drawn Trams of Cambridge.

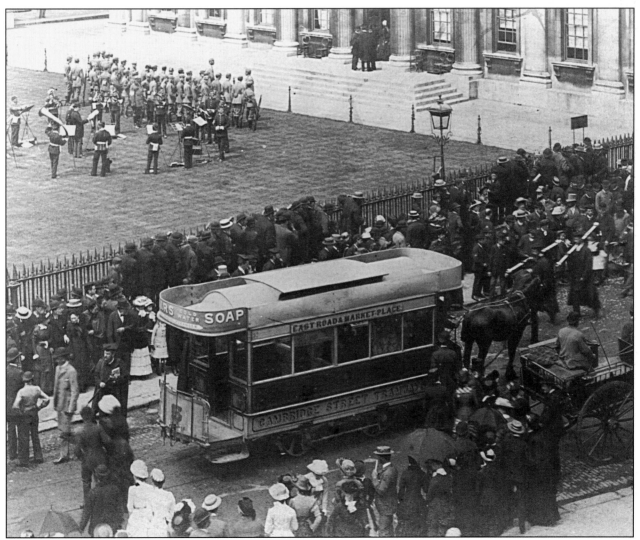

CAMBRIDGE
UP TO DATE!

Motor buses *(below right)* were first seen on Cambridge streets in 1905. By 1906, plagued by technical problems and fears about safety *(above)*, both the motor bus companies had gone out of business. A year later the Ortona bus company began operating, and by 1910 was travelling outside the town boundary. The Tram Company collapsed in February 1914, its last journey accompanied by undergraduates chanting a funeral dirge.

The first half of the 20th century saw bus companies mushroom. Whippet was formed (1919), with Burwell and District (1922) and Premier Travel (1935). With the introduction of the Road Transport Act in 1931 the Ortona company was taken over by Eastern Counties. The present city bus company, Cambus, was formed after national restructuring in 1984 and bought out in 1986 by a management team.

Proposals for a bus terminus at Drummer Street *(far right)*, its present site, were opposed by a 1,000-signature petition and a march on the Mayor's house. It opened in 1925, and by 1947 was already the subject of complaints about overcrowding. Redevelopment was approved, after long debate, in 1985.

Taxis: Hansom cabs *(left)* were hit hard by buses and trams, and again in 1908 with the introduction of motor taxis *(below)*. Attempts to improve the image of the cabs – Sunday working, rubber tyres and, in one case, a performing horse – failed to save them. In 1926 motorcycle taxis were introduced but ousted by Trojan motor taxis in 1927. Radio controlled taxis came to the city 20 years later . . . the first in the country.

Bicycles: By 1910, 42 years after Howes Cycles built the first 'boneshaker' in Cambridge, bicycles were an essential part of city life. The 1920s saw university dons riding bicycles of unusual height and construction. A Regent Street cellist had one with tyres twice the normal diameter to protect his instrument from bumps on the road.

Herbert Robinson, *(below & bot-* *tom)* was doing a brisk trade by 1911. In 1938 the shop took delivery of 500 cycles just before a bus strike. Some cyclists were famous for speed and in 1907 Arthur Markham held world cycling records; whilst Arthur Skeel *(far right)* won cycle races at every distance from ¼ mile to 200 miles and broke the record for cycling between London and King's Lynn in 1912.

A.R. Skeel, on his successful record ride, London to Lynn and back. Leaving Club Headquarters *Toronto for Lynn* Sept 29 1914

9 A.M.

Cycle Clubs like the Wanderers, seen above left in 1902, flourished. In 1913 cycleways were suggested, and in 1925 cyclists were allowed to travel against the traffic flow when Market Street and Petty Cury were made one-way. By 1938 the cycle-versus-car war was well under way with the appearance of a cartoon calling for a ban on motorists. In 1971 450 cyclists staged an anti-car demonstration, but four years went by before new proposals for cycle lanes were put forward; and such demonstrations have been repeated more recently *(left)*. In 1980 a cycle route was opened from Arbury to the city centre, and cyclists were later allowed to use some footpaths.

C ars: Early Cambridge motor-
ing *(above & below)* . . . The
first car arrived in Cambridge in
1897, a four-seater single-cylinder
Peugeot driven by a young undergraduate named C S Rolls, who was
later to team up with a Mr Royce to
manufacture the world's best-
known cars. Seven years later the
city had 113 motorcycles and 42 cars
and 202 licensed drivers.

Undergraduates were mainly to blame for early traffic congestion *(left)*. By 1914 they owned 138 cars and 454 motorbikes. Eleven years later Freshmen's cars were banned, and 1930 saw a total ban on undergraduate motor transport. The Second World War saw a reduction in traffic, but by 1951 there were only slightly fewer cars than in 1938 and commercial traffic had doubled.

City cyclemakers King and Harper became involved in the motor trade *(below)*, and helped young Rolls by repairing the undergraduate's motorised tricycle. The job inspired King and Harper to attempt its own tricycle. The company fitted one with a De Dion engine in 1899 and later converted it to a four-wheeler which won a gold medal at the 1902 Crystal Palace exhibition.

By 1923 Cambridge Motors Limited, whose Cherry Hinton Road premises are seen above with 'the 250,000th Ford car', was designing and building car bodies. The Marshall group began in Brunswick Gardens in 1909, moving to Jesus Lane in 1912.

V̲ictoria Bridge *(below)* was opened in 1890 at the start of the motor age, and was soon funnelling thousands of vehicles into 'Mitchams Corner'. Proposals for a second bridge met with opposition. But after an inquiry in 1965 Elizabeth Way bridge was given the go-ahead.

Several houses had to be demolished and 67 gardens were affected by the building project, which was inspected by city councillors *(left)*. Where Elizabeth Way roundabout now stands was once a quiet junction on Newmarket Road *(above right)*.

The bridge was opened by 1971 . . . providing a river crossing which had been envisaged as early as 1899.

Proposals to improve road links with Newnham were made as early as 1899 with a plea for a bridge from Lensfield Road. Coe Fen Road was finally constructed in 1926 to provide work for 90 unemployed men.

Opposition to the project was typified by the verse shown here:

'The road,' *he* said, 'will be straight and grand,
 With cast-iron railings on either hand,

Concrete conduits, and bridges wide,
 With faked stone walls on either side.'

I shuddered to think of the changing fen.
God! What shall we do with these wicked men?

There was also opposition to proposals in 1930 for a ring road from Trumpington Road. The section from Coldhams Lane to Ditton Walk was finished apart from a final coat of tarmac before the Second World War intervened and work stopped *(below)*. Post-war priorities had changed and it was felt that the outer by-passes would not generally be necessary in the following 20 years and sections were dismantled. Twenty years later the link between Newmarket Road and Coldhams Lane was finally finished. This is a view down Barnwell Road towards Coldhams Lane.

Chesterton Road, Cambridge

East Road seen above right before it was dualled along with Newmarket Road in 1963. Similar plans for Victoria Avenue were rejected.

A similar fate attended the 1949 Holford Report proposals for various inner relief roads, including one from Christ's Pieces to Huntingdon Road – 'a dual carriageway which would split the city'. Later 'railway route' proposals by Buchanan were also dropped. After a major inquiry the northern by-pass was built and opened in 1978, followed by the western by-pass, the M11, two years later.

In 1897 the *Cambridge Daily News* campaigned successfully against plans to allow Emmanuel College to close Emmanuel Street in exchange for new land for another road. By 1906 road gangs *(left)* were laying tar on outer roads to cope with motor traffic. Garrett Hostel bridge and Burrells Walk were closed to motorbikes in 1912.

A one-way traffic system for Market Street and Petty Cury in 1925 was extended in 1936 to the Market and Guildhall area, and in 1947 to St John's Street, Trinity Street and Green Street.

Above right: Road widening in Sidney Street in 1960 to help traffic flow. In 1986 it was narrowed to restrict central traffic.

Other measures to cope with traffic included the introduction in 1934 of the supposedly 'undergraduate proof' Belisha beacon. Between January and April 1955 34 were stolen.

Roundabouts: For a year in 1915 an experimental wooden roundabout was carried each day to the junction of Victoria Avenue and Chesterton Road. In 1932 the roundabout known as 'Milton Road merry-go-round' became permanent *(above far left),* but needed replacing with a new layout in 1967.

The first traffic lights at the bottom of Castle Hill in 1927 'required extra police to keep crowds back and attend to accidents', said the *News*. Eventual acceptance saw them spread to Bridge Street where the road was widened *(below).*

Early parking problems (above left) ... New Square carpark (above), now grassed over, was opened in 1932 to take the pressure off overcrowded Drummer Street. In 1947 the Lion Hotel yard was proposed as a parking area (left), and during 1949/50 was used by 80,000 vehicles.

Right: Undergraduate pranksters found their own solution to parking by putting an Austin Seven van on top of the Senate House in 1958. It had to be cut up before it could be removed.

The first multi-storey carpark, at Park Street, opened in 1963 and a year later parking meters were introduced, emptying the streets as cars queued for alternative parking. Double yellow lines appeared in 1965, and in 1969 parking was prevented at Market Hill and meter charges doubled causing such chaos that police used emergency powers to control the traffic. Two years later both Queen Anne and Lion Yard multi-storey carparks were open.

One Answer to The Parking Problem

VAN ON SENATE HOUSE ROOF

A UNIQUE answer to the Cambridge traffic problem was found during the week-end. Somebody, obviously with an acute parking problem, decided that all the flat space on top of the Senate House was going to waste—so they decided to park an Austin 7 van there!

Early morning passers-by on Sunday goggled and stared in amazement at the strange sight of hefty firemen and policemen struggling to make the van safe from the wind.

It was parked during Saturday night-Sunday morning and it is believed that whoever put the van on the roof made use of some of the equipment left behind by workmen carrying out Senate House repairs.

Who was responsible? Nobody seems to know—or wants to know. But as this is University May Week when anything can happen (and sometimes does) anybody's guess is as good as his neighbours.

This morning the big problem was: "How do we get it down?"

A senior Cambs. fireman suggested the van should be dismantled; it is engineless, anyway.

It would appear to be a problem which should be referred to the engineering department at the University?

It is understood that no attempt will be made by the University authorities to remove the van until some time to-morrow.

"LION" MISSING.

Since Friday the "Lion" has been missing from the Red Lion, Grantchester. An undergraduate 'phoned Mr Frank Rowe, the landlord, and told him that it would be returned in two or three days. The undergraduate did not give his name.

DRIVER'S PRECEDE

American To Pay £27

A 22-YEAR-OLD medical student, of 7519th U.S.A.F. Hospital, Wimpole Park, Leslie Gerald Smith, pleaded not guilty to two offences at the County Magistrates' Court on Saturday. He was represented by Mr. A. M. T. Rose.

Smith was fined £12 for driving at Barton on May 3rd without due care and attention; and £10 for failing to stop after an accident, in which

Photos "Cambridge Daily News."

Top—The van as it appeared to passers-by early on Sunday. Centre—A close-up view showing its precarious position on the ridge of the roof. Below—Firemen lower it to a safe place—still on the roof.

Shopping

The End of Term

Tradesmen depicted begging for end-of-term settlement of bills with an undergraduate *(left)*. Many shops existed solely to serve the university and closed during vacations.

In 1889, Joshua Taylor, put up for sale in 1987, rebuilt their Sidney Street premises. Other stores, Robert Sayle *(below)* and Eaden Lilley, were already well established by then. Competition came from Hallack and Bond, who also chose 1889 to build on the corner of

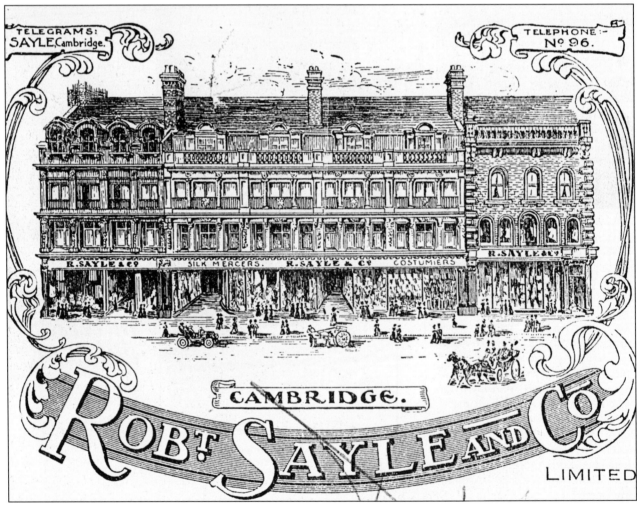

TELEGRAMS: SAYLE, Cambridge.

TELEPHONE: No 96.

R. SAYLE & Co   SILK MERCERS.   R. SAYLE & Co   COSTUMIERS   R. SAYLE & Co

CAMBRIDGE.

ROBT SAYLE AND Co

LIMITED

Market Street and Petty Cury (*right*). The years between the two world wars saw Sainsburys (1925), Woolworths, Marks and Spencer (1934) and Boots open in the centre.

Retailing giant, Matthew and Son, whose advertisement in the *Cambridge Chronicle* in 1922 is seen here, closed in 1964 after 134 years in business. That year Tesco opened its store in St Andrews Street and by that time there were only three locally owned shops remaining in Petty Cury.

Sausages, Pork Pies, etc., Fresh Daily.

Cooked Meats, etc., for Cold Luncheons.

HALLACK & BOND, Ltd.

Family Grocers

TEA AND COFFEE SPECIALISTS
AND PROVISION MERCHANTS

Hill, CAMBRIDGE

Deliveries to all parts of the Town

Telephone: No. 770.

THE XMAS SHOPPING CENTRE.

MATTHEW & SON, Ltd.,

The Stores, Trinity Street, Cambridge.

See our NEW DEPARTMENT

When Shopping The Café, 14, Trinity Street, for Luncheons, Teas, Iced Cakes, Chocolates, Bon-bons, etc.

Grocery Department. Glass and China Department. Art Department. Fleet of Delivery Vans. The Café, Trinity Street. Luncheon Room. The Café, Trinity Street. Provision Department. Wine, Spirit and Cigar Department. Fruit, Flower and Vegetable Department. A Corner of the Despatch Department. The Café, Trinity Street. The Old English Tea Room.

Meat and poultry proudly displayed on Christmas 'Show Night' outside a butcher's shop. In their endeavours to put on the best display some butchers killed more meat than they could sell.

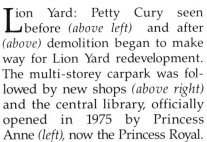

Lion Yard: Petty Cury seen before *(above left)* and after *(above)* demolition began to make way for Lion Yard redevelopment. The multi-storey carpark was followed by new shops *(above right)* and the central library, officially opened in 1975 by Princess Anne *(left)*, now the Princess Royal.

The three Rs, 'rents, rates and recession', began to hit many old-established small traders in the late 1970s, and within the past decade many have vanished. Barrett's china shop *(right)*, established in 1782, left in 1987. Others which disappeared included Bacon, tobacconist, in 1984, Owen Roe, Pigotts, Gallyons, and Bays and Son, King's Parade hatters.

Multiple retailers have continued to expand, but in 1987 a report said Cambridge was doomed as a shopping centre unless a solution could be found to parking.

Fitzroy Street, Cambridge   Valentines Series

Second centre: Fitzroy Street, seen below left before the advent of the car, is part of Cambridge's 'second shopping centre'. After a disastrous fire Laurie and McConnal built a magnificent new store in 1903, and expanded throughout the 1920s and 30s.

Above left: The Forester's Arms pub, which was on the corner of Burleigh Street and Fitzroy Street, in 1890. Ten years later the Co-op moved to Burleigh Street, and in 1930 opened a huge store behind and to the left of the pub *(above)*.

The inadequacy of the shopping area in the historic city centre was noted as early as the 1950s. Redevelopment proposals in 1965, as Laurie and McConnal modernised its frontage and reaffirmed its faith in the area, caused uproar.

In 1977 the store closed, blaming indecision over redevelopment.

Right: Views of the 'Kite' area before and after it became the Grafton Centre. Development was achieved only after long and acrimonious public debate. The result is a new £27 million shopping centre.

Supermarkets appeared in 1963 with the Co-op opening the largest in the county on Milton Road. In 1970 a bulk discount warehouse on Coldhams Lane was converted to a retail outlet. After a public enquiry into planning objections the Beehive *(below)*, as it now is, was allowed to continue.

Sainsburys went ahead with its Coldhams Lane hypermarket in 1973, followed by Tesco at Bar Hill in 1974. After a flurry of new superstore development plans the Co-op began a £6.5 million expansion at the Beehive in 1987, and Sainsburys began to expand at Coldhams Lane.

Mill Road, seen in the early part of this century *(above right)*, was by 1890 the place to buy anything from a piano to a tombstone. Elsewhere, Mitcham's, the shop which opened in 1909 and gave its name to the traffic bottleneck corner, closed in 1977 unable to afford modernisation.

Right: The travelling store of furnishers J H Cooper in 1910. The business, which still operates from premises in Newmarket Road, was one of many which traded in the streets . . . like the hot-cross-bun seller *(above)* in 1911 who started shouting his wares – 'one a penny, two a penny' – at 5.30 in the morning. By 1915 there were no halfpenny buns.

Mill Road, Cambridge.

Aircraft

The earliest aircraft constructed in Cambridge was the Wallbro, built in 1910 by a Mr Wallis. Exhibited at the Mammoth Show the same year, it was destroyed when the hangar collapsed . . . but recreated in 1981 from technical notes published in the *Cambridge Daily News*. In 1964 a pioneering Wallis descendant designed the autogyro which featured in a James Bond film.

The year after the Wallbro's birth, Second Lieutenant W B Rhodes Moorhouse landed on Parker's Piece when he ran out of fuel. He attracted large crowds at other times *(main picture)* when he returned to buy a pair of shoes.

Flying displays over Cambridge began in 1912 with a visit by W W Ewen's Flying Circus, and in 1914 when Gustav Hamel looped the loop in an air show over Rock Meadows, Cherry Hinton.

An air pageant in 1929 marked the opening of Marshall's airport and flying school at Whitehill Farm, Newmarket Road, where it remained until the opening of a new airfield at Teversham Corner in 1938. The company's military work *(inset)* involved it in overhauling and repairing bombers and fighters in the Second World War and converting Hercules for inflight refuelling during the Falklands conflict.

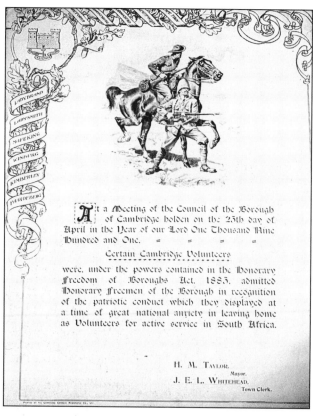

At a Meeting of the Council of the Borough of Cambridge holden on the 25th day of April in the Year of our Lord One Thousand Nine Hundred and One.

Certain Cambridge Volunteers

were, under the powers contained in the Honorary Freedom of Boroughs Act, 1885, admitted Honorary Freemen of the Borough in recognition of the patriotic conduct which they displayed at a time of great national anxiety in leaving home as Volunteers for active service in South Africa.

H. M. TAYLOR, Mayor.

J. E. L. WHITEHEAD, Town Clerk.

War

South African war volunteers returning to Cambridge in 1901 were granted the Freedom of the Borough (*left*) and a memorial was put up on Gt St Mary's Church. Earlier, the relief of Mafeking was celebrated with a huge bonfire on Midsummer Common (*below*). Another on Market Hill marked the relief of Ladysmith.

Two years before the outbreak of the First World War the King stayed at Trinity College (*below right*) while inspecting extensive army manoeuvres near Cambridge. The exercise was marred by two aircraft deaths and an airship accident.

Right: Part of the huge tented encampments for troops which sprang up on Cambridge commons in 1914. Residents supplied hot water and food for the soldiers.

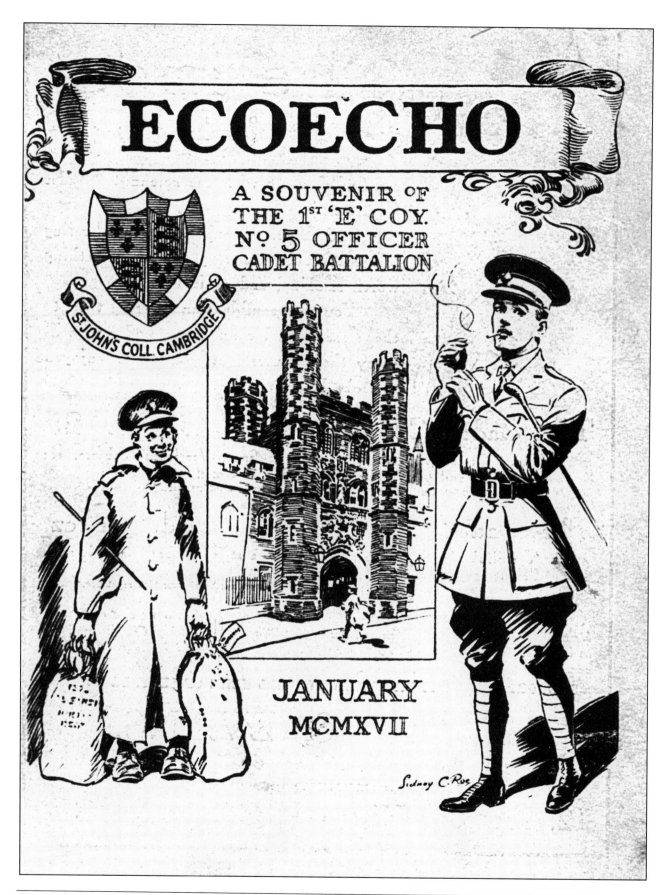

ECO ECHO

A SOUVENIR OF THE 1ST 'E' COY. No 5 OFFICER CADET BATTALION

ST. JOHN'S COLL. CAMBRIDGE

JANUARY MCMXVII

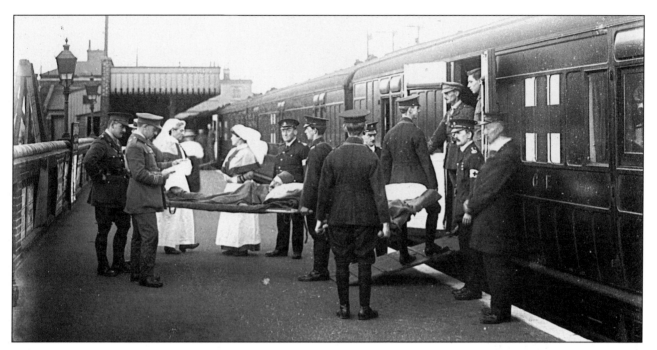

Undergraduate numbers declined during the war. Several colleges provided accommodation for officers in training *(left)* at the rate of 8s. (40p) a day for meals and a room. The move annoyed lodging-house owners also facing a decline in trade.

The First Eastern General Hospital *(below,* at Trinity College) was established to deal with the influx of war wounded. Prefabricated buildings were erected off West Road and hospitals accommodating up to 800 patients continued until the end of the war, with more than 80,000 wounded being transported via Cambridge railway station *(above).*

Armoured cars on Market Hill in 1915 *(left)*, and a year later on the same spot, Sir John French inspecting a parade of the Volunteer Training Corps and Serbian boy refugees *(below)*.

Youngsters queueing for food in Cambridge as the war caused shortages *(right)*. The dangers posed by crowds meant distribution of margarine being moved to the Corn Exchange. Communal kitchens were opened and a food depot and dining room established in Fitzroy Street.

Crowds celebrate the Armistice *(below)*. In Hills Road a temporary war memorial was unveiled in 1922. The permanent memorial was not ready.

The peace movement was active in Cambridge in the inter-war years, and in 1937 the anti-war group issued a booklet on air-raid precautions. But as the international situation deteriorated the Nazi salute was given at the war memorial by members of an Anglo-German contingent *(right)*. German ex-servicemen laid a wreath with Nazi emblems to commemorate First World War dead.

As the war clouds gathered, children were issued with gas masks *(below)* and trenches were dug on Midsummer Common. Lloyds Bank strongrooms were used as shelters and public shelters opened under Peas Hill.

With the outbreak of war university laboratories became involved in research on aircraft gun turrets *(right)*. By 1940 90 per cent of early evacuees to Cambridge had returned home, preferring bombs to boredom.

Fifty-one Cambridge homes were demolished and over a thousand damaged *(above)* in a series of bombing raids. Nine people died when Vicarage Terrace was hit on 18 June 1940. Two years later incendiaries straddled the Bridge Street area killing three people. The Union Society building was set ablaze, 10 buildings were demolished and 127 others damaged.

A vigorous appeal for a volunteer defence force, later the Home Guard, was accompanied by the arrival in May 1940 of two thousand .303 rifles. July saw eight thousand more come from the United States. Jan Ter Braak, later revealed as a German agent, was found shot dead in Christ's Pieces air-raid shelter. A portable transmitter was discovered at his lodgings.

Inset, right: American troops in Cambridge. *Main picture:* The American Military Cemetery at Madingley opened just before D-Day. A model of the invasion beaches was constructed at St John's College.

The honorary freedom of the city was granted to the Cambridgeshire Regiment, imprisoned by the Japanese after the fall of Singapore, and to the 8th US Army Airforce.

At the same time the 'Cold War' saw the start of the anti-nuclear movement. In 1981 peace campaigners staged a mass 'die-in' outside the Guildhall.

UN·SEATED!

CAMBRIDGE BOROUGH ELECTION, 1910.

A.H.PAGET (CONSERVATIVE)   4667
S.O.BUCKMASTER (LIBERAL)   4081
CONSERVATIVE MAJORITY.   586.

Politics and Demonstrations

Freedom of speech: 1910 . . . and the National Union of Women's Suffragette Societies *(left)* is established in Green Street. Three years later, their struggle for the vote escalated, and violence involved setting fire to a house in Storey's Way and damaging the gates of St John's College.

A cartoon from 1910 *(below left)* depicting the Conservative parliamentary candidate, A H Paget, unseating the Liberal S O Buckmaster, and regaining the seat for the Tories. Labour contested the seat for the first time in 1918 but only won the seat twice, in 1945 and in 1966. MP Robert Davies *(below right)* died within 15 months of entering the Commons, and was succeeded by the Conservative David Lane *(right)*, now Sir David, who was followed by Robert Rhodes James *(below)*.

Undergraduate volunteers, like those pictured below, left Grange Road in fleets of cars in 1926 to maintain essential services like the railways during the General Strike. Left-wing politics flourished during the inter-war years. The early 1930s saw Guy Burgess, later exposed as a spy, and other undergraduates join hunger marchers from Newcastle en route to London; in 1936 another group stayed at the Corn Exchange.

Far right: RAB – Lord Butler, with Lord Adrian, Dennis Healey and Harold Macmillan, at the Cambridge Union. Other postwar speakers at the Union included Harold Wilson and Enoch Powell. The 1960s and 70s saw student protest grow over Vietnam and other issues.

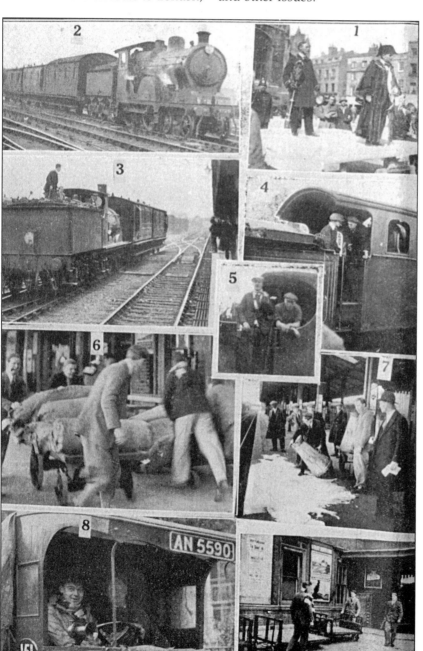

Student violence *(top)* culminated in 1970 with a riot at the Garden House Hotel, where a dinner was being held to mark a Greek Week. Six were jailed by Judge Melford Stevenson, who described the episode as 'the most complete example of intelligent young people getting involved in complete bloody nonsense'. By 1984 the university's proctors were disappointed at the lack of student

dissension and blamed political apathy.

Above: A cartoon showing police guarding their city headquarters in 1904 as undergraduates tried to rescue a colleague arrested during a running battle with mounted police on Parker's Piece. At one point police were forced to defend the Christ's Pieces bandstand to prevent it being destroyed.

Rag Day bicycle 'streaker' *(below)* . . . the first Poppy Day Rag was in 1922, and thousands of pounds were raised by the Rag over the years for the Earl Haig Fund. The mid-1960s saw the city tire of student Rag Day stunts which ended in fighting between students and local youths. By the late 1970s, after a series of flops, the Rag was taken over by the Cambridge Students' Union and is again raising money for a number of charities.

Bonfire night: Rowdy Bonfire Nights *(right)* causing hundreds of pounds worth of damage were traditional until the early 1960s.

The early 1900s saw 'chariots of fire' . . . blazing hansom cabs which were driven around Market Hill. In 1948 a hand grenade was thrown at the Senate House and rockets aimed at the Guildhall clock.

May Week – traditionally held in June since 1882 – includes May Balls, boat races on the Cam and concerts, and marks the end of the academic year. It was described in 1904 as 'the brief week in which the permanent part of the population takes much coin of the realm from the floating part' *(far right)*.

Police and Fire Services

Cambridge police force had been established for 52 years by 1888. Until 1897, police headquarters *(below)* rubbed shoulders in St Andrews Street with the Spinning House, where the university imprisoned prostitutes. The Spinning House was in that year handed over to the borough. Four years later it was pulled down and new police and fire headquarters were built on the site, remaining in use until both forces moved to Parkside in 1970.

Right: The county jail on Castle Hill, which closed in 1916. The gallows were last used in 1913. An open day before demolition in 1930 attracted 8,000 visitors to the prison.

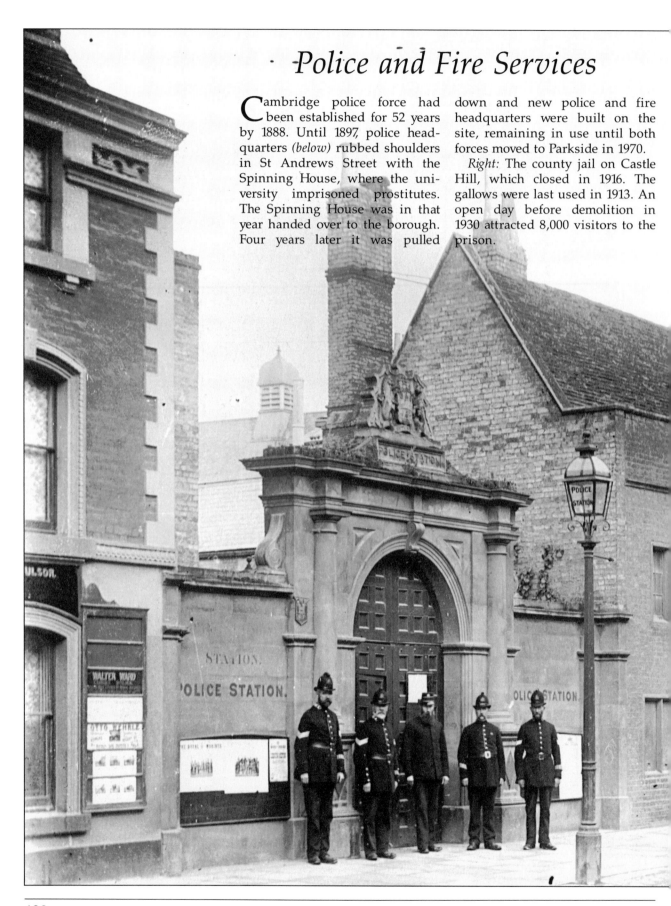

The early 1970s brought a new problem . . . soccer violence. In once incident in 1981 51 people were arrested. Following another outbreak in 1984 three men were convicted and jailed at the Old Bailey.

Between October 1974 and June 1975, the police were involved in the city's biggest ever manhunt – for an attacker who was to become known as the Cambridge Rapist. Peter Cook was eventually caught and jailed for life.

BITS OF OLD CAMBRIDGE

No 7   THE FIRE BRIGADE

CAMBRIDGE
FIRE BRIGADE

Cambridge has seen some spectacular fires. In 1914 Watts timber yard was destroyed. A similar fire at Ridgeon's yard in 1984 caused £750,000 worth of damage. 1890 saw the biggest fire in the town in 30 years at Clare College. In 1928 hundreds flocking to watch Grantchester Mill burn down *(above)* blocked the road. The Garden House Hotel was destroyed in 1972, and in 1976 a blaze at Brights Building, Magdalene College, was described as the worst for years.

The city's fire service has come a long way since 1903 when a fire at Laurie and McConnal's store threatened the whole of Fitzroy Street because of the absence of a fire engine. In 1906 a steam fire engine was in use *(left)*, but the lack of horses meant firemen had to pull it themselves. It was 1920 before a motor fire engine was bought *(above left)*. In 1984 American Chevrolet rescue tenders *(right)* were introduced.

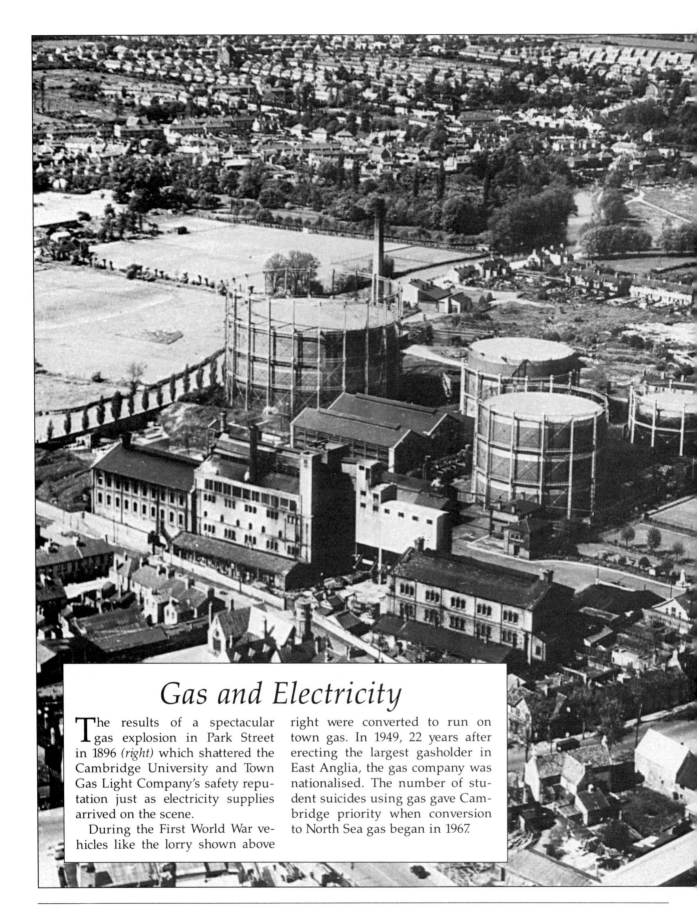

Gas and Electricity

The results of a spectacular gas explosion in Park Street in 1896 *(right)* which shattered the Cambridge University and Town Gas Light Company's safety reputation just as electricity supplies arrived on the scene.

During the First World War vehicles like the lorry shown above right were converted to run on town gas. In 1949, 22 years after erecting the largest gasholder in East Anglia, the gas company was nationalised. The number of student suicides using gas gave Cambridge priority when conversion to North Sea gas began in 1967.

The first public electricity supply in the town came from a dynamo in the basement of Baily, Grundy and Barratt's shop in Great St Mary's Passage. In 1892 Cambridge Electric Supply Company was established with large steam turbines at Thompson's Lane *(above right)* and substations like this one on Market Hill *(right)*. At first the company operated only at night. The national grid mains reached Cambridge in 1927, twenty years before the 250-volt system was inaugurated. Conversions were not completed until 1972.

River Cam

The river saw heavy commercial use in the early part of the century *(left)*. Until 1914 the steam cargo carrier *Nancy* made regular trips between Cambridge and King's Lynn. In 1906 H C Banham began boat building at Riverside, and in 1911 introduced the famous *Viscountess Bury* pleasure cruiser *(right)*. In 1976 the business moved to Ely, and a marina at Logans Way closed in 1981 as unprofitable. The Cam also acts as a skating rink when conditions allow, as in 1894, 1929 and here in 1963.

BANHAM MARINA

The old highback bridge at Jesus lock *(below right)* which was replaced in 1892. College bridges, like St John's Bridge, the Bridge of Sighs *(below)* and the old Garret Hostel Bridge, 1890 *(overleaf)*, demolished in 1960 and later replaced, offer an attractive way of crossing the Cam.

Ferries *(right)* were slow and unreliable. In 1904 De Freville Estate residents agitated for a bridge at the Fort St George crossing. The town council agreed in 1913, and it was finally erected in 1927. One ferry survived, at Fen Ditton, until 1961 when it sank after being overcrowded during the Bumping Races.

Sport

Rowing *(below left):* In 1888 an undergraduate died in the 'Bumps' when his heart was pierced by the pointed bow of another boat. In 1892 another was hit by lightning. Seven years later, YMCA members barred for smoking set up their own club, the '99.

The river was also a popular swimming venue. Cambridge Amateur Swimming Club was formed in 1906; it was followed in 1934 by Granta Swimming Club, which organised an annual swim from Grantchester Mill to Sheeps Green. Later the route was changed and now swimmers start from Mill Pool and swim along the Backs *(left).*

Twelve years after the opening of Parkside swimming pool in 1963 the Kelsey Kerridge sports hall opened next door, providing a venue for sport and other events.

Cricket: Fenners, the home of university cricket was bought in 1892. In 1927 in a Varsity v Middlesex match, K S Duleepsinhji scored 254 not out. Seven years later the great Don Bradman was bowled at Fenners for a duck. Nearby Parker's Piece *(below)* was the training ground for many famous cricketers, including Jack Hobbs, whose name is commemorated in the pavilion erected in his honour in 1930.

Football, also played on Parker's Piece, grew after 1902 with the formation of the Cambridge and District Thursday League.

It was another six years before Cambridge Town Football Club, now Cambridge City, got under way. Abbey United, now Cambridge United, started in about 1910 playing on Malta recreation ground in Romsey Town until the Abbey Stadium opened in 1932. Both clubs were elected to the

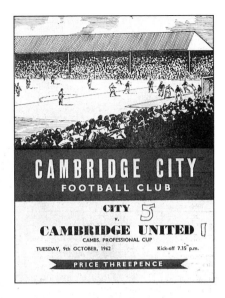

Southern League in 1958, and played against each other. The programme shown here was for a game in October 1962.

United was admitted to the Football League in 1970, and has since enjoyed varying success, at one stage reaching the second division.

Cambridge Evening News

The *News* was the first evening newspaper in Cambridge . . . and has remained the only one.

It was the brainchild of William Farrow Taylor, who came to Cambridge from Bury St Edmunds. Its early years were a struggle, and it depended heavily on its sister paper, the *Cambridge Weekly News,* later to become the *Cambridge Independent Press* after engulfing a rival.

The present *Weekly News* series of nine newspapers remains a major part of the Cambridge Newspapers group, which serves an area 25 miles around Cambridge.

Under Mr Taylor's third son, Captain Archibald Taylor, a mayor of Cambridge, chairman of Cambridgeshire county council and at one time president of the Newspaper Society, the *News* continued to flourish. In 1929 it was sold to a national group later known as the Amalgamated Press, in which the first Lord Iliffe, head of the family who are the proprietors to this day, had an interest. Captain Taylor stayed on as managing director until 1960, by which time the *News* had come wholly under the control of the Iliffe family.

Since its move in 1962 from St Andrew's Street *(above)* to its present site in Newmarket Road *(right)*, the paper has switched to new technology. By 1986 most of the typesetting was being done by journalists using computerised input.

ARCHIBALD TAYLOR LORD ILIFFE ROBERT ILIFFE

MORLEY STUART
. . . 31 years as editor

H H HIGGINS
. . . 1949-64

The editor's chair was occupied successively between 1888 and 1903 by Mr Townsend, Mr Mac-Arthur and Mr Stanley Jones. His successor was A Rought Brooks (1903-18), and then for 31 years Morley Stuart led the editorial team. H H Higgins (1949-64) was followed by Keith Whetstone, one-time president of the Guild of Editors, later to be editor of the *Coventry Evening Telegraph* and editor-in-chief of the *Birmingham Post and Mail*. Nicholas Herbert, now Baron Hemingford and editorial director of the Westminster Press group, edited the *News* from 1970 until 1974 after working for *The Times*. He was also president of the Guild of Editors. His successor was Colin Webb, also a *Times* man. He left in 1982 to return to *The Times* as deputy editor, and is now editor-in-chief of the Press Association. For 18 months Stuart Garner, formerly deputy editor of *The Journal*, Newcastle, took charge. He moved to Norwich in 1984 as editor-in-chief and director of Eastern Counties Newspapers. The present editor, Robert Satchwell, is a former Journalist of the Year and assistant editor of the *News of the World*.

KEITH WHETSTONE
. . . later at Coventry and Birmingham

NICHOLAS HERBERT
. . . 'Times man'

COLIN WEBB
. . . now at the Press Association

STUART GARNER
. . . in charge at Norwich

ROBERT SATCHWELL
. . . the eleventh editor

IAN RICHARD
. . . arrived in Centenary year

There have been fewer managing directors. Captain Taylor was succeeded in 1960 by Mr A J H Durham, a past president of the Young Newspapermen's Association who has been active in the Newspaper Society and the Commonwealth Press Union. He relinquished the post at the end of 1987, handing over to Mr Ian Richard.

The present chairman of Cambridge Newspapers Ltd is Mr Robert Iliffe, who succeeded his uncle Lord Iliffe in 1975.

The family is also involved in newspaper publishing in Birmingham, Coventry, where it founded the *Coventry Evening Telegraph*, Burton-on-Trent and Falmouth.

A J H DURHAM
. . . managing director for 27 years